AF580008

LET'S BEHAVE

NO MORE BULLYING

By Darlene Gardner

LET'S BEHAVE
NO MORE BULLYING

Printed in the United States

By Darlene Gardner

ISBN 978-1-7328735-3-7 (Hard Cover)

ISBN 978-1- 7328735-4-4 (Ebook)

Library of Congress Cataloging-in-Publication Data is available

1 2 3 4 5 6 7 8 9 10

First Edition

In Loving Memory of My Mother

Lucy Lee Gardner,

who taught me to treat others the way I want to be treated.

I will love and honor her always

It was just after breakfast Auntie Darlene and the children were all sitting around the lesson table, when the doorbell rang. Auntie Darlene went and opened the door. It was Kaitlyn.

"Good Morning Auntie Darlene!" she said as she rushed past her.

Auntie Darlene could hear the children shouting, “Hi Kaitlyn!” as she closed the door. A few seconds later, she could hear yelling. It was Parker and Christian.

“What’s wrong!?” asked Auntie Darlene.

“Kaitlyn stepped on me and Parker,” said Christian.

“My feet were right here, and Christian’s feet were right there,” said Parker.

“And then, Kaitlyn walked right here and stomped her feet on me and Parker,” explained Christian.

"Kaitlyn, did you step on Parker and Christian?" asked Ms. Darlene.

Kaitlyn nodded and said, "Yes."

"What should you have done?" prompted Ms. Darlene.

"I should say 'excuse me,'" said Kaitlyn.

"Why didn't you?" asked Ms. Darlene.

Kaitlyn hunched her shoulders and said, "I don't know."

"Then you need to apologize to your friends," said Ms. Darlene.

"Okaaay. I'm sorry," said Kaitlyn.

When Ms. Darlene went to get the lesson sheets, Kaitlyn sat down at the table, spreading her arms wide, elbowing the two children sitting beside her.

"Auntie Darlene, Kaitlyn is pushing Christian and me with her elbows," said Parker.

"Kaitlyn, that is not the way we sit at the table," said Ms. Darlene. "Please sit up. You are being rude to your friends."

"Okay," said Kaitlyn.

"WHAT TIME IS IT?" yelled Ms. Darlene.

"IT'S LESSON TIME," yelled the children.

After passing out the lesson sheets, Ms. Darlene turned around to write something on the blackboard. Kaitlyn snatched Parker's lesson sheet and threw it to the floor.

"You're going to get in trouble, Kaitlyn," Ms. Darlene could hear Parker saying.

“What is going on?” said Ms. Darlene.

“Kaitlyn took her paper,” said Auggie.

Parker stood up after attempting to pick up her paper, which Kaitlyn had placed her foot on top of.

“Parker, are you okay?” asked Ms. Darlene

“Kaitlyn threw my paper,” she said, as she pointed to the paper on the floor. “And she has her foot on it.”

“Parker, you can sit down,” said Ms. Darlene. “Kaitlyn, pick up Parker’s paper, hand it to her, and apologize for taking and throwing it on the floor.”

Kaitlyn was not very happy about having to pick up the paper or saying sorry. She placed the paper on the table, folded her arms across her chest, and muttered, "Sorry, Parker, for throwing your paper down."

"Kaitlyn, I am very disappointed in your behavior. It was very rude and disrespectful to behave that way," said Ms. Darlene.

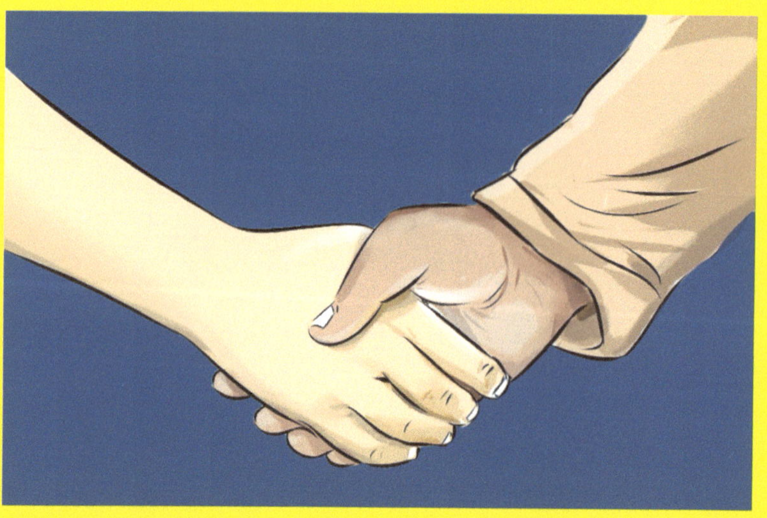

“I want to talk to you all about ‘bullying,’” said Ms. Darlene. “Does anybody know, what a bully is?” she asked.

The children all looked around at each other. None of them knew. They all shrugged their shoulders.

“In a short time, some of you will be going to big kid school. You’ll be going to Kindergarten,” said Ms Darlene. “Do any of you have a big brother or sister in big kid school?” she asked.

“My brother Alextheo goes to big kids school,” said Christian.

“My sister Marlie goes to big kids school too,” said Marlan.

GAP

“Big kid school is much larger than daycare. There are a lot more kids there,” said Ms. Darlene. “You will be able to make a lot of new friends. Who is going to make the most new friends?” said Ms. Darlene.

“I’m going to make a lot of friends,” exclaimed Parker.

“Me too,” agreed Christian.

“I know how to make a lot of friends,” said Marlan.

“How do we make friends?” asked Ms. Darlene.

“We just say, ‘Hi,’” said Marlan.

Ms. Darlene smiled and said, “Yes, we say hi.”

“Kaitlyn, are you going to make any new friends?” asked Ms. Darlene.

“I don’t know,” she said.

“Don’t you want to make friends?” asked Ms. Darlene. “What if you get to Kindergarten, you meet a little girl, and she takes your backpack and throws it down? Do you think she can be your friend?” Ms. Darlene asked.

“No, she’s being mean,” said Kaitlyn.

“She’s rude,” said Marlan.

"Isn't that what you did to Parker?" asked Ms. Darlene.

Kaitlyn nodded and said, "But I didn't mean it." She looked at Parker and said, "I'm sorry, Parker. I didn't mean it."

"That's alright," said Parker.

Ms. Darlene explained that a bully is someone who treats others badly. “They threaten or hurt others who are smaller or weaker than they are. They try to make people do what they want them to do, or play what they want them to play, or else they become angry.”

“Is Kaitlyn a bully” asked Marlan.

“If the girl who takes Kaitlyn’s backpack is a bully, and Kaitlyn takes Parker’s paper, then Kaitlyn’s a bully too,” said Christian.

"Bullies act tough, and they act tough so people will be afraid of them. Bullies like people to pay attention to them and to think they are special," Ms. Darlene explained. "Does anyone know how to stop someone from bullying them?" asked Ms. Darlene.

"You hit them back," said Parker.

"Well, first we try to stay away from the bully," said Ms. Darlene. "If a bully sits next to you at school or outside, and he or she tries to make you do things or is threatening you, try to move away from them. Tell them 'I'll be right back,' and then find another friend to play with. You can also tell your teacher, or if you're outside, find an adult. And don't forget when you get home to tell your parents."

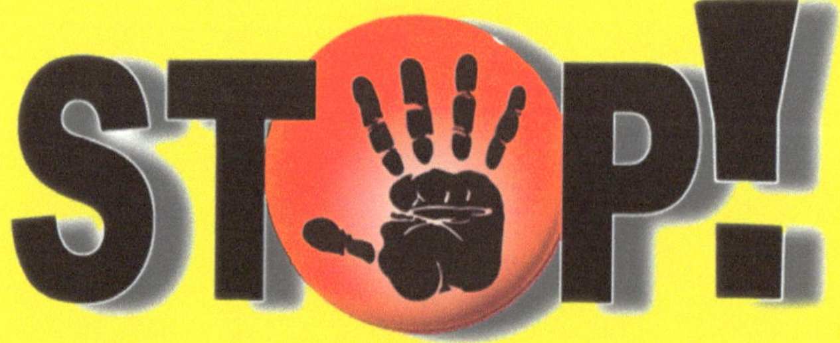

"I'm going to stay away from bullies," said Parker.

"I'm going to be nice to my friends," said Kaitlyn.

"If we want to have friends, and we want people to like us, we have to treat people nicely. Nobody wants to be friends with someone who hurts them or makes them feel bad," explained Ms. Darlene.

"I'm sorry for making you feel bad, Parker," said Kaitlyn.

"That's okay," said Parker.

DEAR PARENT

Bullying is in our schools, parks, and neighborhoods. There used to be a time when parents only worried about their children being bullied at school, but now it is everywhere.

It is important that we talk with our children about bullying and how to deal with bullies when faced with these difficult situations.

NO MORE BULLIES

- Be kind to others
- Stay away from bullies
- Find an excuse to get away from a bully
- If you are at school tell an adult or teacher if someone is bullying you
- When you get home tell your parents

CPSIA information can be obtained
at www.ICGtesting.com
Printed in the USA
LVHW072156090322
713080LV00007B/26

* 9 7 8 1 7 3 2 8 7 3 5 3 7 *